PUFFIN BOOKS

DEAR ANNE FRANK

Anne Frank was born in Frankfurt am Main in Germany in 1929. During the Second World War the Nazis occupied Holland, where Anne and her family had fled, and created a police state. The Nazis believed that some races, such as Jews and gypsies, did not deserve the right to live. Because Anne and her family were Jews, they were afraid they might be killed, and went into hiding. During this time in claustrophobic captivity Anne wrote a diary which chronicled her thoughts and experiences. Near the end of the war the hiding place was betrayed and the occupants were deported to concentration camps, where Anne died of typhus in 1945, a few months before her sixteenth birthday.

After the war Anne's diary was published by her father, Otto Frank, the only surviving member of the family. It became a bestseller all over the world, and has been published in more than fifty languages.

To commemorate the fiftieth anniversary of Anne Frank's death, Puffin Books and the Anne Frank Educational Trust UK together invited schoolchildren to take part in a letter-writing project. They were asked to imagine that they could post a letter through time to the secret annexe in Amsterdam where Anne wrote her diary: what would they like to say to her? There was a marvellous response, and thanks are due to everyone who took part.

This is a collection of letters and extracts chosen from the many thousands of entries.

Dear Anne Frank

PUFFIN BOOKS

PUFFIN BOOKS

Published by the Penguin Group
Penguin Books Ltd, 27 Wrights Lane, London w8 5tz, England
Penguin Putnam Inc., 375 Hudson Street, New York, New York 10014, USA
Penguin Books Australia Ltd, Ringwood, Victoria, Australia
Penguin Books Canada Ltd, 10 Alcorn Avenue, Toronto, Ontario, Canada m4v 3b2
Penguin Books (NZ) Ltd, Private Bag 102902, NSMC, Auckland, New Zealand

Penguin Books Ltd, Registered Offices: Harmondsworth, Middlesex, England

Published in Puffin Books 1995
5 7 9 10 8 6

Filmset by Datix International Limited, Bungay, Suffolk
Printed in England by Clays Ltd, St Ives plc
Set in 11/15 pt Monophoto Bembo

Introduction

When I met Anne Frank in 1940 we were both eleven years old. Before we all had to go into hiding our two families lived in the same square in Amsterdam. I well remember Anne playing in the street. She was not a goody-goody – she was an ordinary happy girl, a little precocious perhaps, but looking forward to life's richness and challenges. Her life was extinguished, like that of many others, because of the insane theories of the Nazi regime.

In 1953 my mother married Otto Frank, Anne's father. He had survived Auschwitz concentration camp and so had my mother and I, by a series of miracles. Otto's family, my father and my brother had perished. In 1957 my stepfather created the Anne Frank House in Amsterdam. This is the house in which the Frank family had been hiding for two years. Otto intended it to be an educational institution, rather than just a memorial. He believed in the power of education to prevent what had happened to our families happening to others.

On reading Anne Frank's diary, many thousands of children from all over the world were moved to write to my stepfather, Otto, and it became an engrossing full-time occupation for him and my mother to answer each and every one of them personally.

Fifty years have passed since the death of Anne, who would have been my stepsister. Sadly we cannot say that there has been no more persecution. The Anne Frank Educational Trust UK, of which I am a Trustee, is becoming recognized as a major force in the education of Britain's youth. Our touring exhibition, 'Anne Frank in the World 1929–1945', has been visited by over 500,000 people and it continues to travel all over the country. The purpose of the exhibition is to alert young people, especially, to the consequences of racism, prejudice and discrimination.

Anne Frank's greatest wish was to become a writer. Indeed she was – not just a writer, but a magnificent chronicler of the human spirit in all its moods. The number of beautiful heartfelt letters written to her for *Dear Anne Frank* reflect the power of her personality, which has survived the fifty years since her death.

I am therefore delighted to have been involved in this project, and congratulate Puffin Books on this wonderful and timely event. The letters addressed to *Dear Anne Frank* come from children of all faiths, colours and cultures, and show that it is precisely this human diversity which enriches our lives and which we should value highly. If we do, Anne will not have died in vain.

Eva Schloss
1995

The Anne Frank Educational Trust UK

The Anne Frank Educational Trust UK is a non-political multifaith educational charity committed to preserving the legacy of Anne Frank. It is the only British organization licensed by the Anne Frank House, Amsterdam, to use the name Anne Frank for educational purposes.

For further details of its educational projects and for membership write to:

The Anne Frank Educational Trust
Garden Floor
43 Portland Place
LONDON W1N 3AG
Registered charity no. 1003279

The Holocaust must never be forgotten and its warning messages for today must never be underestimated.

The Letters

A Life in Hiding

The hardships and restrictions of Anne's life in hiding, as well as the restrictions placed on all Jews by the Nazis, touched a nerve with many letter-writers, who tried to imagine how they might have coped in similar circumstances.

Dear Anne,

I found a copy of your diary in a box in the roof which belonged to my mum. The book fell open on Saturday 20th June 1942 and so I read the entry. What was it like in the Second World War? Was it scary?

When I read the entry I was disgusted and surprised at the way that Jewish people were treated under Hitler's anti-Jewish laws. How did Jewish people cope with it all? What would happen if you broke some of the rules? Who would tell on you and why? You must have felt someone was watching and waiting for you to do something wrong so they could report you. I would hate handing my bike in. I would hate to think of someone else riding it around. It was my best Christmas present. I couldn't go riding with the scouts. I would really miss that.

If my father had to lose his car and was not allowed to drive or to use public transport, he would lose his job. He would not get such a good job in Bewdley so the family would have less money. It would have been very hard doing your shopping between 3 p.m. and 5 p.m. because all the best things would have gone. I know what Sainsburys can be like at the end of the day. Did the shopkeepers keep some nice things back for the Jews?

I would not like on a sunny evening, to be indoors from 8 p.m. and not even allowed to play in my own garden after that time. It would stop me from playing with friends and going to scouts.

If I were banned from going to a theatre, cinemas and other places of entertainment I would not have seen pantomimes, plays, many films, seen Phil Collins in concert, been ice-skating, go-karting, and to laser quest. I can't imagine not being able to play sport or go to the swimming pool as I enjoy these so much.

Were you ever tempted not to wear the yellow star that told everyone you were Jewish? And your life would have been so much easier but it would be denying your Religion and all it means to you.

I cannot imagine how you coped with all these restrictions and many more that came along. I think you must be a very strong and determined young lady. Be brave and strong and don't let the regulations get you down.

Best wishes,
from David Mills

David Mills (age 11), Worcestershire

Dear Anne Frank,

I think that you and your family were very brave hidden in the annexe. If I had been hidden I think that I would have been caught straight away because I am a very noisy person with a loud voice, and I always fall out of my bed. It must have been terrible not getting outside, and not being able to walk, or talk, in the daytime. It must have been boring tiptoeing about and whispering. What did you do all that time? You and your sister must have got on well because Dawn (my sister) and I always fight and argue.

I have read your diary. It is good. You tell me your feelings about the war really well. When I was reading it, it put me in your shoes and made me think how it would have been. I understand how hard it must have been for you.

Yours,
Kimberley Paterson

Kimberley Paterson (age 11), Motherwell

Dear Anne,

I think it hard to believe that someone as young as you could be deprived of freedom. You could no longer sing or skip as I can, no longer stamp or slam doors when in a mood. Not live a life of a normal teenager. When I read your diary I see how you are full of life and happy before the war. You remind me of me on the 12th of June. I too would wake up hours before any one else on my birthday, just waiting for my presents.

Adolf Hitler talked of a perfect race, to me a perfect race is for everyone in the world to get along no matter what colour or what religion. We may not all be the same but we are equal to each other.

Yours sincerely,
Eleanor Jeffery

Eleanor Jeffery (age 11), Cleveland

Dear Anne Frank,

I have been looking at the plan of the house where you are hiding. It must be like jail in there. It must have been boring having no friends. It would be horrible having dry bread to eat and porridge and lettuce. I would like to be able to bring you some fresh vegetables and cake and chocolate biscuits.

Yours sincerely,
Matthew Waddington

Matthew Waddington (age 7), North Yorkshire

Dear Anne,

I hope you are not angry with me or other people of my generation for moaning about minor details like we haven't got anything to wear to the disco on Saturday night or we can't afford to go swimming and to the cinema on the same night. I do feel guilty sometimes when I complain that I have to be home by 10.30 p.m. instead of 11 p.m. at week-ends, some of my friends aren't allowed out at all and you had no choice, you had to stay in that small cooped up room for two years. Here in Britain teenagers have a brilliant life compared to some people in other parts of the world but the reason we are not always grateful for it is because we don't know any different, it's just a way of life for us.

From what I've read about you, you were obviously a normal teenager, you seem to have liked the same things as we do today: music, films and boys. I can't imagine having those things taken away from me, I wouldn't be able to cope.

I'm glad to say that a few things have changed now, there are still wars between countries but people's personal opinions are different, people respect each other, no matter what race, and are learning that your skin colour or what you believe in doesn't matter, it's what kind of person you are inside that counts.

Yours sincerely,
Helen Savage

Helen Savage (age 15), Kent

Dear Anne,

It must have felt really sad moving because you would have missed all the things in Germany. I would have felt really sad if I'd had to move. I live in Thamesmead. Thamesmead is in the south-east of London and I wouldn't like to move. I would like to read your diary and go to your secret annexe. It makes me feel sick that Hitler killed six million Jews. You must have felt sad that innocent people were going because they're Jews. I'm Chinese, and I know how it would have felt if Chinese people had to die because they're Chinese.

I'm glad your dad was clever. Anyway I am so sad that you ended up going into the concentration camp and you died. I hope you can hear me.

Yours sincerely,
Nancy Nim

Nancy Nim (age 11), London

Dear Anne Frank,
The only way I could have coped with the voluntary
imprisonment you had to suffer was to treat it as an
adventure.

I would have drawn and played card and board games to
pass the time. But being in the same rooms as my brother
for two and a half years would have driven me crazy!

If I had to be shut up in a room for that long nowadays, I
would take my electronics set with me, to make gadgets.

Best wishes,
Craig

Craig Robert Banham (age 11), Norwich

Dear Anne Frank,

I have read your diary and found out you are very much like me. You like boys – I do as well.

I thought you were very brave when you were hiding. If it was me I would be very scared and helpless. I would never talk in case I would be found out and I would never move around I would just sleep. I wouldn't be as brave as you.

Anyway I have a disabled brother called Paul. We couldn't keep him quiet because sometimes his wheelchair creaks and he can only crawl around. If he crawled round you could hear him coming because sometimes he bangs when he crawls around.

My sister and me just fight all the time so we couldn't keep quiet. My mum and dad are OK with me. We sometimes argue but sometimes they are sound. I suppose we could be quiet.

Anne you are very brave. If it was me I couldn't leave my family, friends, neighbours, but I suppose you had no choice. Life today is so different. I wish you could be here now.

Leah Stott

Leah Stott (age 13), Birkenhead

Dear Anne,

We have been learning about special people and on the 13th of October Mrs Dawson our teacher told us the story about you and your family.

I think it was ever so cruel of the Nazis to drive you out of your own country and make you wear those yellow stars. If I had my own way I would give that Hitler a piece of my mind. When Mrs Dawson told us the story it brought tears to my eyes. I think your father was a very brave man when he took you into hiding.

I do not know why the Germans did it. You are only humans like us.

Mrs Dawson told us about the young boy Peter and that when you went into hiding you didn't like him at first but then you started to love him. I would have thought that he would have loved you too because you were a very attractive girl.

I wish I could have met you and been your friend.

I think I'd better go now. Bye.

All the best,
Stacey Rowland

Stacey Rowland (age 10), Sheffield

1.   When Mrs Van Daan moans about her teeth try to ignore her.

2.   At all times ignore Mr Dussel.

3.   If he tells me to be quiet tell him SHHHH!

4.   Try to keep quiet and not move around when the workers are here.

5.   When Margot gets praised try not to get upset.

6.   If Peter calls me names start singing or hum.

7.   Be more friendly with mother.

8.   Even though we haven't got much food think about the people outside, we have a lot compared to other people.

9.   When the sirens are going keep calm . . . .

Kate Widdowson (age 12), Hagley

Dear Anne Frank,

How was life in Germany? I hope it wasn't too bad. It must have been horrible at the concentration camp. I know how it felt in the war. You are lucky to play out in the street – I'm not allowed to even put my foot out without my mummy. What kind of food did you eat in the concentration camp? It must have been crowded in the hideout with eight people. I wouldn't like to stay in a hideout staying quiet for two years. Why did you call your diary Kitty?

from
Toby Vacher

Toby Vacher (age 6), Bristol

Dear Anne Frank,

I wonder how you felt in your Annexe. I don't think that it was very nice. Did you name it Annexe because your name is Anne? Was it hot or cold? When your sister got the letter, did you expect it was about going to a work camp? Was it boring being quiet from 8.30 til 12.30 and quiet again at 14.00 til 17.30? How did you feel when you could move around in the evening? I think I might have felt ill.

from Karl Antony Raistrick

Karl Antony Raistrick (age 7 ½), Bradford

Writing Diaries

Some writers chose the subject of diaries as their theme – and many were concerned about how Anne might feel if she knew that so many people had read her private thoughts. This invasion of privacy was, in fact, something which troubled Anne's father, Otto, and he thought very hard about it before going ahead with the diary's publication.

Dear Anne,

We have just been reading your diary in English and have enjoyed learning about you.

Do you mind people reading your secrets? I read your diary in class without a thought of you not wanting me to. Between friends, if one friend read another friend's diary then surely they would no longer be friends and the diary reader would know all the secrets and private things, the hopes and dreams that the diary writer had shared with this book. But still your book, your personal diary, was shared with the whole world. Did they ever stop and say 'Maybe Anne wouldn't want us to know her secrets?' But maybe you don't mind.

I just don't understand how you could have coped. I am twelve and even though I am not as grown up as some of my friends, I am still nosey and love to use the telephone! I have only been sitting writing for twenty-five minutes and already I need a change of scenery – so I'll leave it at that.

Bye for now!

Yours,
Emily Kernick

Emily Kernick (age 12), Exeter

Dear Anne Frank,
I wanted to talk to you on the subject of diaries!

You see, I also keep a diary but when I read yours I realized how very different it was from mine.

My diary was a Christmas present four years ago. I can still remember the little parcel wrapped in shiny, gold paper lying under the Christmas tree. Unlike you, I have to admit I was a little disappointed when I opened the parcel to find a plain, brown book. My spirits were hardly lifted by the blank white pages staring at me when I opened it! I was very much into 'Turtles' that year so if a package didn't contain a 'Donatello' or a 'Michelangelo' I wasn't really interested. I remember thinking 'How boring' when I opened the parcel – well, I couldn't have been more wrong . . . could I?

I first wrote in my diary in the summer of 1992 – fifty years after you began yours.

It seems that you were writing most days between the years 1942–1944 but I only keep my diary when I am on holiday. Your writings took place in a small, secret room where you were hiding, often feeling tense or afraid. I have been lucky enough to write in many different and wonderful places where I enjoyed so much fun and freedom.

On August 4th–9th 1943 you told 'Kitty' about a typical day in the Annexe – the usual routine of getting up at quarter to seven, listening to the BBC in the afternoon but never going out, of course. On those same days just over fifty years later I was writing about an exciting trip to China with my parents, walking on the Great Wall, flying from Beijing to Nanjing, standing on a bridge looking down at the mighty River Yangtze . . . don't we tell a different story! I have never known what it is like to be shut away from the world, I have never known what it is like to hide in fear, I have never known long hours of silence where I was afraid to even turn on a tap.

Although both our diaries are packed with details of what has happened to us – those details are worlds apart, as they say, and while my story will only ever interest me and perhaps my own family, yours will always fascinate the whole world.

Yours,
Philip

Philip Straughan (age 11), Cleveland

Family Experiences

Some letter-writers spoke of the lives of their own families during the Second World War and described how Anne's diary had given them a helpful insight into their relatives' experiences.

Dear Anne Frank,

My grandmother is the same age as you were. She is Greek Orthodox and she lived in Greece (which was also invaded) during the war. When the Germans invaded she hid messages for the Greek Rebellion. She told me that she hid them by folding them up and pushing them into the place between the spine and the cover in her Encyclopedia so when soldiers came to search her house and they opened all the books and shook them nothing happened. Her brother was executed for being part of the rebellion. He already had a wife and a two-year-old son (who is now my sister's godfather). Sometimes I see my grandma sitting and staring with tears in her eyes. I ask her what is wrong and she answers, 'I am just remembering.'

With love,
Allie Huttinger

Allie Huttinger (aged 11), London

Dear Anne Frank,

I am an eleven-year-old Jewish girl and I feel very strongly against the Nazis and Adolf Hitler because my grandma was taken to a concentration camp and might have been killed if it hadn't been for Schindler, and Schindler only saved her because her brother worked for him and if a person worked for Schindler the rest of his or her family were allowed to work for him too. He would let them work for him for a small sum of money, lots of people were saved this way.

Every time we remember the war I am scared that it might happen again and that more people will be killed. Sometimes I think that I might not be alive today because of Hitler. If my grandma had been killed my mother would never have been born. I sometimes have dreams that Nazis will rule again, and people that never did anything wrong will be killed in concentration camps again just like you were. On remembrance day the whole country of Israel remembers the people who died in the Second World War. When the horn goes everything stops, even cars in the street. Sometimes I feel like I want to cry because the rest of my grandma's family were killed in the war, and while others have great-grandparents, I have none.

Yours sadly,
Avital Maisel

Avital Maisel (age 11), London

Dear Anne,

You don't know me, but I guess that's the point. You never knew anyone for the last two years of your life. You must have been really stressed out! I guess you just had to get used to it . . .

To be absolutely honest, I feel slightly guilty. The reason is because my grandad fought for the Germans. Don't get me wrong, he never wanted to – he was forced. If he wasn't in that war, he wouldn't have been shot in the leg or been split up from my grandma for as long as they were. I'm sorry, and I'm sure he is too.

Forever thinking of you,
Jo

Joanna Hartmann (age 14), Leicester

Dear Anne Frank,

I cannot begin to tell you how much your diary has taught me about your life. I have learnt a lot about the war but living in the 1990s in safety, I cannot possibly know how it must have felt living in such a scary situation. I am also Jewish and my grandparents have also been through the same horrific times that you did. It was such a painful memory for them that they find it very hard to talk about it. Many of my family were killed as yours were and I have only a few great-aunts and uncles left alive now. It upsets them a great deal to mention it and I would never dream of pressing them for information. That's why it's so nice for me to be able to read your diary without upsetting you and to learn from your personal thoughts. I am very interested in the war and its effects on individuals. Being thirteen is not a lot different from my age and I feel that I am reading something I could have written about if I'd lived in that period.

Yours faithfully,
Lauren Cohen

Lauren Cohen (age 11), Buckinghamshire

Poems

Some of the letters were in the form of poetry. Here are three of them.

Dear Anne,

Hiding from the Nazis,
Hiding in the roof,
You know one day they'll get you,
You'll have to face the truth.
Up some stairs,
Behind some books,
You've found a place
Where no one looks.
A washroom with no windows,
No shower, just a sink.
Mustn't speak to anyone,
Must cut off every link.
An attic room upstairs,
The nicest place in there.
It's only got one window
To let in cool, fresh air.
Cooped up in a hiding place,
Same people every day.
Must begin to tire of them,
Just want to get away.
Only got a few things
The favourite things you've got.
Should I take my red frock,
Maybe – maybe not.
Hiding from the Nazis,
Hiding in the roof,
You know one day they'll get you,
You have to face the truth.

Tom Weeks (age 13), Norwich

Dear Anne Frank,

The bombs scare me in the dark.
The guns scare me in the dark.
The dog barks scare me in the dark.
Noises scare me in the dark.
People taking me away scare me in the dark.
Shadows scare me in the dark.
Soldiers scare me in the dark.
The robbers make noises. It scares me in the dark.
I wish the Germans hadn't taken your bike that was horrid.

from Wayne

Wayne Brooks (age 7), Somerset

Dear Anne Frank,

'Dear Kitty'
You used to write,
As you wished
To fly a kite.
You really wished to be outdoors
And go and play on the see-saws.
You used to hear the soldiers march
And write it in your book,
But when they took you away
The diary they never took.
But now your dad has published it
So other people can know
And see how bad it really was
Fifty years ago.

Sharon Jacobs (age 8), Hertfordshire

Letters from the
Past and the Future

Some writers chose to imagine themselves living in the 1940s, or as characters in Anne's life, such as Kitty, the imaginary friend she wrote to in her diary, or even the unknown individual who eventually betrayed the Franks' hiding place. One writer imagined herself caught up in a war in the future, too.

Dear Anne,
My name is Noel Smith. I live in a little passage under
ground. It's very damp and each night I'm very dirty. We
burst a pipe and water comes out of it so we can wash
ourselves. There's a little gap in the ground so we can get
some light. This is my address in code: _._.._ __ ..._!...*.
I've got a few questions to ask you. How long roughly do
you look out of your window? I normally look through the
gap. How many pages do you write each day in your
diary? I normally write one page. How many rooms and
people are in your hideout? I've only got one big room and
two brothers, a mother and a father. Please write back.

from Noel Smith

Nick Ian Persich (age 9), Suffolk

1 Rodney Street, Germany

Dear Anne,
Hi, I am Laura Walker, I live at 1 Rodney Street in
Germany. Please don't put the letter down – read it. I am
not like the other Germans, I think it is dreadful that they
put you in a death camp. How would they like it if the
British people came along and put them in a death camp?
But the British people wouldn't do that. I wrote to you
because of all the dreadful things that the Germans are
doing to you and the rest of the Jews. If I could, I would
take Hitler to a death camp and see how he likes it. If I was
at the death camp I would be very scared. Try not to
worry. I am sure Britain will win and you will be free from
that horrible place. I hope I can come and see you sometime.
I wish you luck.

Laura Walker

Laura Walker (age 10), Grangemouth

Dear Anne,

I am sitting here in my small bedroom, trying to imagine what it must be like for you, sitting in your small bedroom.

When I have finished writing to you, I can go downstairs. I can go out, I can sing and shout – or cry, but you . . . you have to stay quiet. You can't talk or even move around in case someone hears you.

How do you manage, day after day? I don't think I could do that. You must be brave. I would be scared. Scared that I would be discovered and sent away.

You know that Jews are sent away, just because they are Jews. Are the rumours true? Do they really kill them? I worry for you Anne. Please be careful. Promise you won't try and go out. Stay quiet a little while longer. Stay safe a little longer. Stay alive a little longer.

Sonia Vine

Sonia Vine (age 13), Cleveland

Dear Anne,

I am really sorry that your family has been sent to the concentration camp! I think I owe you an explanation! It was me that betrayed you. You might not know who I am, because you have never met me before, but I've met you.

I betrayed you because you were a Jew, I just didn't care who you were. I am sorry that this has happened, it is because Hitler said that he would exchange a Jew for money. At the time, my family needed money desperately. Without money, my parents could not survive from their illness.

The only way I can get the money is by betraying you. I did not really want to, but I love my parents so much. When I saw the army dragging your family out of the building, I felt really guilty. If I did not feel guilty I would not be writing to you. I know you will never forgive me for this, I am not expecting you to, I just want to tell you I am very sorry.

from
Angela

Betty Wong (age 14), Cleveland

Dear Anne,
Hello, how are you?

I feel very odd walking down the streets with a yellow
badge showing that I'm a Jew. Everyone looks at you as
though you're not a human being. They are burning all the
Jewish books in front of a book store. We're not allowed to
go to the cinemas, not even allowed to touch a bike and
worst of all, we're not allowed to go to school. We have to
whisper in our apartment that we're sharing with another
Jewish family. I heard that Peter is moving in with you. I'm
moving to a big building and living at the back of it. I have
to eat the same things – I'm getting sick and tired of it but
it's better than nothing. How's your family? Mine's worried.
As I might not survive this war, this is the last letter you
will be receiving. I hope your special dream comes true of
being a writer.

Best wishes,
from your friend,
Reshma Soni

Reshma Soni (aged 10), Surrey

Dear Anne,
It must be terrible being locked up in an attic like you. I'm sure I would have the wobbles. I have read your diary and it's very sad. I wish you could come to England and be safe. I bet it is very cold and boring in the attic and I bet you can't get any sleep at night. I bet it's very frightening. I hope you can stay there a little bit longer and be safe.

Love from
Lara

Lara (age 8), Middlesex

Dear Anne Frank,
I think that you are a bit bored, so I am going to do you a word search. I hope you will enjoy it. It is going to be words like war and Anne and things like that.
This is it:

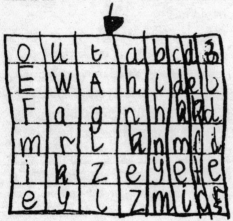

Anne
war
soldiers
hide
out
eye

from
Rachel Berry

Rachel Berry (age 8), Blackburn

Dear Anne,

I know this letter will come as a complete shock to you, especially as you were in hiding for two years, but during those two long years I was your closest friend. Every day you confided in me how you felt – your feelings, your hopes, even your feelings for Peter. Your frustration at not being able to scream out loud after confrontations with others, everything you told me.

Just how did you cope? For a young girl I think you coped better than most adults would have. You rarely let yourself go and you very rarely cried. You were so brave coping with the fear of being found – even though I think you knew it would happen, you willed it not to. During those two years you grew up at a remarkable rate. You realized that your carefree schooldays had gone. When you first went into hiding you had fits of crying, you were lonely, you wanted Pim to help you. Help you make the transition from young girl to young adult but he couldn't.

Alone you had to face the task of changing. To realize the responsibility of adulthood all in a few days. This is hard enough for anyone, but with the added pressure of hiding from the Nazis, I don't know how you did it.

You wrote that you thought that no one was totally evil, that everyone had some good in them and that one day the world again would see peace. It makes me sad and angry that you never lived to see that day. If anyone deserved to survive that war, it was you. You were brave, hopeful and responsible and over the years, and for many more to come, people have respected the young girl who never once lost hope and always believed good would triumph.

All my love,

Yours,
Kitty

Gareth Williams (age 15), Cleveland

Dear Anne Frank,

It is now the year 2026 and we have entered World War Three. Of course the conditions of this war are very different from yours. Britain and central Europe are at war with America and China. I am not in hiding like you but I can relate to a lot of what you said in your diary. Our war is equally as horrific as yours, innocent women, men and children suffer horrible disfigurements and painful deaths caused by radioactive bombs. At first I had given up on our world, but your story touched me and gave me a new hope for the future.

You are far braver than I ever was and reading your diary inspired me to do as much as I can to help others, even if it's just being a bit more tolerant with those around me. I know, in some way, I will be making life for them easier.

Mainly, though, I am writing to say thank you. Your story stopped me from feeling sorry for myself. I wish with all my heart that your story could have had a perfect ending but unfortunately we do not live in a perfect world.

Yours sincerely,
Katy Saunderson

Katy Saunderson (age 14), The Wirral

The World Today

World events since Anne's death were the focus of many letters, as well as comparisons between her world and the world as it is today. However, views differed greatly on whether or not 'progress' has been made.

Dear Anne Frank,

It's now fifty years since you died and your diary is being ranked among the works of Shakespeare and other great writers. It is studied in schools by many students all over the world including me. You will be pleased to hear that Hitler lost the war, which was so big it was even bigger than the First World War. For this reason it's called World War Two.

Even through these hardships man has not yet learned not to kill. In Bosnia a similar thing is happening with Serbians ethnically cleansing the Muslims, causing a lot of bloodshed. What's worse, the governments say they are paying attention to doing things, but in fact they are not. Reporters taunt the injured by constantly asking questions about relatives who have died, bringing back sour memories. They also say they're sending in armed forces to deal with the problem, as if the killing of an opponent is better than a peace treaty signed.

Some good developments happened after the Second World War. Israel was formed, a state for the Jews to call home. But it wasn't formed with the Palestinians' permission, who lived there earlier. This mistake caused years of war and unrest which has only just begun to end.

It has become a hard world since you died, but a better world since Hitler was defeated.

from
Matthew Butler

Matthew Butler (age 13), London

Dear Anne,

Hi. My name is Hannah, I'm thirteen years old and I am Jewish. You wrote in your diary that you wanted the world to be good, and for everyone to love one another, well everybody who reads your diary feels the same way.

Since I was about nine years old, I have read your diary at least twice a year. I too write in a diary, expressing to it all my thoughts and feelings. But yours is special. It is so unique and if you survived the war, I am positive you would have published many thrilling books and done many wonderful things for the world. Now, your book is famous all over the globe and has been translated into many different languages. Every day, thousands of people from all over the world come and visit the 'Secret Annexe' in Amsterdam, which is now known to everyone as the Anne Frank House. There are exhibitions about you and your family everywhere and recently, I saw a wonderful one in St Albans Cathedral – 'Anne Frank in the World'.

As you know, Pim, your father, married again. So you now have a stepsister who I believe you vaguely knew before you went into hiding. Her name is Eva Schloss and she also wrote a diary, except her diary is like a sequel to yours. She actually wrote it all down, years after coming out of a concentration camp. Her diary is very sad and very moving. When I read it, I kept thinking about how awful it all was, and how it was telling me all the bad things that had happened to you, in great detail. But luckily, Eva was one of the few fortunate people who had survived and she is still alive today. I hope the two books will be sold together one day, as at the moment, not too many people know about 'Eva's Story'.

In a way, your diary is like a memorial to the six million Jews who died. Because of your diary, the memory of the Holocaust will live on, from generation to generation, telling everyone that it must never happen again.

Thank you.

Yours affectionately,
Hannah Neidle

Hannah Neidle (age 13), Watford

Dear Anne Frank,
You must have had a lot of courage to stay in the secret
annexe for two years.

The food must have got very unpleasant – kidney beans
every day? My Uncle Alan had baked beans for a whole
year! You must have been tempted to go outside regularly.

Unless you didn't know, did you know that your diary has
become famous? Did you want it to? Why did you call
your diary 'Kitty'? What was being taught by your father
like?

Anyway, changing the subject slightly Hitler is now dead,
and the EEC has been formed. Now Germany is good
friends with us. It was a lot of fuss and bother!

Your diary I found very interesting and I hope England has
caused you no offence. I think you must have been very
organized to write a diary every day.

I do hope you enjoyed my letter.

Yours,
Adam Bach

Adam Bach (age 10), Stafford

Dear Anne,

How could you manage to stay strong through your experience? You didn't once feel down or depressed. You were always so lively and full of fooling. I know I would have gone to pieces, but not you, you kept going no matter what happened.

I would so much like to know more about you, but I know I can't. And I would especially like to know how you felt when the green police found you. I would have been hysterical and would have tried to kill myself. Not you though, you appeared so calm and together. I only wish I was like you.

Life today isn't much different apart from the technology is a whole lot more advanced. But the attitudes have stayed the same. People still are against people with different beliefs than themselves. If there is a racist killing no one really bothers about it, everyone is immune to it now. People only care about themselves, no one else. Every day it's me, me, me. I know you would forgive them Anne, but I can't, I'm just not like you. You always thought people were good at heart. Maybe there are some good people but not too many. Even when you were alive people were bad, and it's no different today. There is crime in every town, city and country in the world. I wouldn't say it was worse than your time, because nothing is worse than the Nazi regime. But it's definitely no better, and as I said before if there is a mass killing or even just a few, none of us lose any sleep over it. That's how bad it is. If only everyone would read your diary and understand it, I think the world would be a lot better. I learned a lot from your diary and I thank you for it.

May your memory live on.

Your friend,
Billy Rankin

Billy Rankin (age 14), Strathclyde

Dear Anne,

There is so much I would like to say to you that I don't know where to begin. Firstly I would like to say that since you were here, nothing has happened to your fellow Jews to make them feel different or unwanted as you were. I also think you should know that your father, Otto Frank, was the only survivor of the war from your hiding place. He made you the famous writer you dreamed of being.

Some time after the war your father appeared in a programme called *Blue Peter* on a thing called a television. A television is like a radio but has a screen and moving pictures as well as sound. *Blue Peter* is a programme on the television.

I have read your diary and done a play about you and now I feel as if I know you.

from
Henrietta LeFroy

P.S. Your diary is the best book I have ever read.

Henrietta LeFroy (age 11), London

Dear Anne,
Since the time you were alive, many things have changed.
Man has landed on the moon, people can now travel faster
than sound, there is an underwater train tunnel joining
England and France, and also you do not have to be
engaged to kiss a boy.

Yours sincerely,
Daleen Begg

Daleen Begg (age 14), London

Anne, my friend, some people don't believe it ever happened, they are convinced that the Holocaust is a lie, and we are getting to the stage where all our survivors and witnesses are dying. The Neo Nazis could easily rise again. I went to the Holocaust Museum in Jerusalem last summer and you'd never guess who was there – you were – and a large printed extract from your masterpiece at the entrance. It is a very horrific but touching place. I went to the children's memorial, a room with five candles reflected cleverly again and again to create thousands of bright star lights representing the children murdered at Auschwitz, the death camp, and as I walked through this room I prayed to God that it should never happen again. It may not necessarily involve Jews, but at the rate we are going – anyone.

Anne, thank you for your gift to this world, it teaches us a great deal about self-discipline and suffering and, as you wished, your soul most certainly lives after your death.

Your friend and admirer,
Amy Racs

Amy Racs (age 13), London

Dear Anne Frank,

My name is Arooj. My teacher read me a bit from your diary and I really enjoyed it. I think I know how you feel about persecution because I have been persecuted too. I went into hiding because some girls shouted some racist remarks at me. I was shopping in the town centre when some girls shouted 'Look at that poor girl,' and 'She's brown,' shouted another. I went home and didn't go to town for a week. I am very outgoing and talkative and I hated being in hiding for a week, never mind two years. I also sympathize with you for eating all that ghastly food, because I'm a fussy eater. I think you are very brave and I admire you.

Yours sincerely,
Arooj Shah

Arooj Shah (age 10), Blackburn

Dear Anne Frank,
I am writing a letter to you to inform you that there is still
a lot of racism.

In my experience white people are teasing the black Asians.
They are teasing us about our religion. They tease us about
our Gods and our places where we worship. I feel so sad. I
wish you were still alive today. I wish you were here to
help me.

Love from
Rekha Ben Ram

Rekha Ben Ram (age 12), Leicester

Dear Anne,
In our life today there are many racist remarks about people
around the world. I just wish people could treat others as
they would want to be treated. Maybe I am asking a little
too much.

Yours sincerely,
Donna Forrester

Donna Forrester (age 14), St Helens

Dear Anne Frank,

Your diary extract about the things that made the Jews suffer made me feel extremely sorry for you. I've experienced not being able to play with your friends that have different nationalities. Every time I want to play football with my friends who live in my flat my father calls me back upstairs. He thinks that they're Palestinians, but they're Pakistani and Indian. Now that's changed. I knew how you felt that time. I also know how you felt giving in your bike, well sort of. I used to have a bike to share with my brother. It got thrown away and now my father doesn't want another because he thinks it's dangerous. I've got over that now, that's all behind me, as I hope you put your dreadful times.

Yours,
Baba M'Boge

Baba M'Boge (age 12), Jeddah

Dear Anne,

Nobody has learned a lesson. There are still lots of people who are fighting for no reason. Two years ago in Yugoslavia the people were putting Muslims in concentration camps. People were throwing grenades in the Muslims' houses. Do you know why they were doing this? They were doing this because they didn't like the Muslims, the Muslims had a different religion to the people living there. This reminds me of a similar situation which you were in.

A few weeks ago we went to the 'Anne Frank Exhibition'. Of course, they had a lot about you in the exhibition and we didn't have time to see everything.

There were some photos of you. There was a photo of you when you were only one day old lying in your mother's arm. Just by looking at the photo I felt sad. You and your mother looked so happy, none of you had any idea about what was going to happen to you in the future. The bad thing which happened to you was that you died but the good thing is that you are still remembered by millions of people in the world because of your diary. You never know, but one day all the wars and fighting might stop. You never know.

Yours sincerely,
Sumeira Aslam

Sumeira Aslam (age 11), Glasgow

Dear Anne Frank,

Nothing has changed since the war. I mean people have walked on the moon, aeroplanes have reached the speed of sound but people are still fighting for the silliest of reasons.

Six million Jews have died because of Hitler. He knew he was in trouble so he committed suicide but the Nazis are still around all over the place. There is the Nazi party – the B.N.P. which is short for the British National Party.

The B.N.P. are trying to get the black people out of Britain and once they are out they will pick on someone else, but they are in a minority. We are going nowhere, are we?

Yours sincerely,
Ross Malcolm Kennedy

Ross Malcolm Kennedy (age 11), Glasgow

Dear Anne Frank,

I am writing to you to tell you that nothing has changed since you sadly left us: 'He who ignores history is condemned to repeat it' – well we must have had plenty of ignorant people because we seem to have repeated history.

I don't mean the odd person taking his or her racist feelings to extremes, I mean organized gangs and racist political parties.

Since the Nazis there has been a number of racist organizations and a number of incidents. In Germany there was a football match cancelled because of threats by Neo Nazis to riot and after that a match arranged in Austria was cancelled because of fears that the German Neo Nazis would pour over the border into Austria and cause a riot there. But the problem is it's not just on the continent of Europe but all over and not just gangs but a political party. In a London by-election the British National Party actually won the election and were set to carry out their policies of getting non Brits out of that constituency. One thing to be thankful for is that at the general election only a short time after that they were knocked out of that seat.

But Anne as you can see life will never change if we ignore history so the way forward is through the past.

Yours sincerely,
Christopher Park

Christopher Park (age 14), Aberdeenshire

Dear Anne Frank,

My name is James Gardner. I am interested in Science, History, Art, English and Mathematics. My hobbies are dinosaurs, cooking and trains. I attend Colfe's Prep School where we are researching into the Holocaust. Today my class mates and I listened to extracts from your diary and I found it very emotional.

I appreciate how terrible your experience must have been. If you do not mind I would like to ask you some questions.

Do you think keeping diaries is a good idea?
Do you think the publishing of your diary will help future generations?
Why was hardly anything done to help you and the other Jews?
What was it like to be locked in a dark room, waiting for the German police to find and take you away to the concentration camp?

Today the evil lives on. Children are still victims of persecution and racism. Children of Northern Ireland do not know whether a knock on the door belongs to friend or foe. Children of Bosnia were killed or seriously injured in a savage war. Children in Rwanda face famine and cholera.

Do you have a message for all the children who suffer today like you did when you were young?

I would be most grateful if you would answer some of the questions.

Best wishes,
James Gardner

James Gardner (age 10), London

Dear Anne Frank,

Today when I got up I yelled at my sister because she was smirking at me and told me that I was stupid because she had got ready before me. It went on for a good ten minutes. It was like a mini war. I've probably forgiven her now, well I will if she's in a good mood when she comes out of school. But if she's in a bad mood I'll be awful to her. Well, she'll be awful to me won't she? Is that how countries' governments act?

I don't know. But it seems like they do. Why do people want war anyway? It doesn't do anything except destroy, and create a brief 'Victory' until the other side rises and there will be war again. War. I wonder what it stands for. World At Riot? Worthless Assorted Ruining? Something like that.

World peace. World eternal peace. Chances of that happening by itself – zero to infinitive. Chances of it happening with us all trying – infinitive to zero. I guess it's time to go and make sure I'm nicer to my sister.

Love,
Alex

Alexandra Palmer (age 12), West Sussex

Dear Anne,

I hope that in the next fifty years, in the next century, things will have changed, improved, then, and only then will the world be a better place to live in. A place where everybody can feel safe and welcome. Where people have learnt to live with each other and respect other people's religions. You and your family and friends had to suffer a great deal because you were Jewish, people still live in fear and hiding now, let's hope that in the next fifty years things have changed and people don't have to live like this.

Yours faithfully,
Sophie Kochne

Sophie Kochne (age 13), London

Dear Anne Frank,

Why is war such a hobby for man? I think it is wrong because it costs so much money and lives, all because people are too greedy and want to rule over more land.

Countries nowadays, I think, spend too much money on trying to make weapons bigger and better and armies bigger and stronger than ever. Although armies like the United Nations try to bring peace it still results in people suffering from deaths in their families.

Lives are too precious to waste on war: they are not like a machine where you can have it mended. When you die you die but some people don't realize this and are too greedy, so they send others to war to attempt to benefit themselves. The way things are going scientists will be eventually making bombs to wipe out countries and even continents.

I think it makes more sense to make peace in less harmful ways instead of killing off the population, and helping other countries. With the money spent on the armed forces every year you could easily help countries like Africa improve their living conditions. This idea of peace would save a lot of pain, agony, grief, money and lives!

Will man ever learn?

from
Stuart Watson

Stuart Watson (age 14), Peterhead

Dear Anne Frank,

Hello, my name is Sarah. I live in Ayr a long distance away from you, but I feel we are quite similar. We both play musical instruments and hate practising. My father is a dentist but he isn't half as touchy as Mr Dussel!

As I said before we have a lot in common as we can both relate to violence. Violence is quite a problem in this world. There are wars all over the world, not as big as what you've had to stand but size isn't the problem, the problem is the reason. I think wars are stupid. Even on children's television there is violence which just encourages younger viewers.

I wish all the children could get together and put a stop to violence! I suppose it's not half as bad as your war but it is a serious problem.

I think the best way to get round this problem is to make ourselves heard! We should write to programmes and newspapers expressing our views. We should also debate in school and tell TV programmes like *Blue Peter* to let the world hear *US*, the children!

Yours faithfully,
Sarah Foran

Sarah Foran (age 11), Ayr

Dear Anne Frank,

Perhaps a campaign, dedicated to your memory, should be started to stop discrimination and racism between children, especially in areas where there are mixed races. We must make them realize that we are all the same underneath. Maybe, if our generation grows up thinking in this way, discrimination and racism will stop before they get out of hand.

Yours sincerely,
Elizabeth Badcock

Elizabeth Badcock (age 13), Surrey

Dear Anne,

Lately, I have been reading a book called *Zlata's Diary*. It was written by a girl living in Sarajevo. She started her diary on Monday, 2nd September 1992, which was just under five months before the war started. Just like you, Zlata writes about how she is 'trapped' in her home, unable to make contact with the outside world. Zlata lived in fear, as most of her family and friends were either wounded or killed. Eventually, on the 17th of October 1993, Zlata and her family were able to leave Sarajevo. They then went to Paris where they could live in peace. You, your family and millions of other Jews were not even given a chance like this. From reading both your diaries, I have learnt just how lucky I am not to be living in a war, fearing for my life.

Many people could learn about how the lives of innocent children are horrifically ruined through war, if they spent time reading your diaries.

Yours,
Joanna White

Joanna White (age 12), London

Anne's Legacy

*Many letter-writers wanted to tell Anne how she had inspired
them personally, and how her legacy lives on.*

Dear Anne,

I feel I must write to you directly to explain my thoughts about your life. After all, that is what people truly celebrate when they read your diary. It is the sordid fact that you didn't make it which saddens people the most; it seems that all your optimism was for nothing. Although it may seem that it is your death which is remembered, I'd like to say to you that this is not the case. People feel inspired by your vivid mind and your will to live through bad times.

When I read your diary I feel as if I am living through it too. I believe that every one of your readers feels you should have lived.

The irony, of course, is that had you lived, your diary would most probably never have been published, at least until your eventual death.

That fact says to some people that your death wasn't totally in vain; something good came of it: that is, many people learned of the true horrors of the Holocaust. Maybe so, but that doesn't compensate in any way for the life of an intelligent, vibrant young girl. If you had lived, people would find out about the Holocaust in another way.

A memorial service was held on what would have been your sixty-fifth birthday. I read at that service. I felt that I was helping in a very small way to prevent another Holocaust.

I can imagine that many people in despair have read your diary and felt uplifted; it has given them the strength and inspiration to battle on.

Rest in peace. You deserve it, dear Anne.

Luci

Luci Verrill (age 15), Cleveland

Dear Anne Frank,

I am writing this letter because I feel the need to say thank you and also to say sorry.

I would like to say thank you, because your life, mirrored in your book, has made people think about war and discrimination throughout time. I know I have.

I would like to say thank you for making me realize the preciousness of freedom; I do not have to leave my house, my friends and live in a secluded house where the slightest noise, the slightest movement out of place could endanger my life and the lives of my family and friends.

I would like to thank you for showing me the true face of war. War is not just about the glory of laying down your life for your country, it is also about ignorance, hate, deprivation, suffering and above all about the denial of peace and love.

I would like to say sorry because you had to go through all that mental and physical suffering having done nothing to deserve it.

I am sorry because you, your family and your friends had to die so that future generations had a chance of learning how to respect the lives and views of other people.

I would like to say sorry because in parts of our world there are still wars, there are still people who are suffering because of their religion and the colour of their skin and it seems as though your lesson has not been learned.

I know I cannot change all that, but I am sure that when our turn will come to run the world we will still remember Anne Frank and that will help us in making sure that nothing like that will ever happen again.

Love,
Anna

Anna Molle (age 13), Watford

Dear Anne Frank,
I think that you are so courageous that if each ounce of your courage was worth a penny you would be a millionaire.

Best wishes,
Christopher Millard

Christopher Millard (age 11), London

Dear Anne,

I feel pretty awful having to write to you like this when I'm just doing work for school and your diary was the outpouring of all you were really going through, locked away in quite literally a few tiny rooms. A captive, completely in the hands of your protectors without outgoings and without any company of your own age to give you a break from your parents.

My life is full and free and though my parents nag me on occasion, I have the variety of school life and weekend interests. There is a certain relaxation in being with people of my own age. We talk about our parents, our pocket money, our leisure interests, our favourite pop group or song. We discuss the latest good film we have seen at the cinema or programme on television.

I know I should appreciate my freedom to live, travel and be governed according to just laws. I shall try not to take these things for granted as I grow up. I would like to help or join Amnesty International which tries so hard to free or raise the spirits of forgotten and abandoned prisoners of conscience.

I will try also not to let the seeds of racism grow within my own attitudes and behaviour or to go along with racism in my friends and companions.

It touches me very much that your bravery never faltered until your sister died. Even you, with all your inner strength, were quite dependent on your sister's companionship. I shall try to appreciate my brother who often tries my patience now, for people tell me that in years to come, he and I will be a strength and support to each other.

Thank you for sharing your experiences with the world.

Yours sincerely,
Gemma Warris

Gemma Warris (age 12), Surrey

Dear Anne,
I am writing to you because I want you to know that you are not forgotten and your short life and death were not wasted. I have read your diary and so have millions of other people all over the world. It is now a book translated into many languages, keeping the memory of the Holocaust alive. If the world remembers then we can stop anything like it happening again.

I know that, now, if I see any racist bullying in the playground I'll stop it!

Yours,
Rowan Lupton

Rowan Lupton (age 13), Aylsham

Dear Anne,

In the end you forgave them. Why? Why did you forgive the men who wanted to take so many innocent people's lives? The victims had done nothing wrong and yet in the end, you forgave the people for the dreadful things they had done.

That is one of the things I could never have done. That is why so many people admire your courage.

Rest in peace dear Anne.

From an unknown friend from the future

Amanda Teichler (age 13), Essex

Dear Anne,

I think this is a little bit weird because I know you are dead but anyway I feel it unfair, me being a Protestant, that Jews were being killed in the millions. I can understand how you felt being locked up in the same place for so long because when you're our age you've got to get out.

I understand that you always get into trouble for trying to make people laugh, but you always end up hurting people. I think you have the same problem as me and ought to keep your lips closed and don't say a word.

I try to work out what you would be like now at sixty-five years old. I think you would be a lot more mature but still wanting a laugh, sort of just like a more mature version of you at fifteen. I wonder if you would still have bitterness to the Germans or if you would have forgiven them but I think you would still hate the Nazis for killing your family and taking all your human rights away.

I think it is good for children our age that your father decided to publish your diary. If you were still alive today everyone would want to meet you and ask you questions.

I think you would have made a good writer today, and you made a lot of people understand more about World War Two. Thank you Anne for writing your diary.

Yours sincerely,
Ross Park

Ross Park (age 12), Glasgow

Dear Anne Frank,

Days are days and as each one passes, I take it for granted. I don't really look at the beautiful wildlife around me, or the beautiful autumn leaves around me swaying in the cool breeze, or even sometimes the people around me. I hide away like a little creature, away from the cold winter days.

But from reading your diary you really inspired me to live my life – to not take every day for granted and also not to hide away all my feelings, and actually talk to someone.

I really respect you for all that you lived through, the bombings and sometimes deaths of close relations and not even knowing if you would live another day or be found out in the 'Secret Annexe'. As every day went past you always enjoyed every moment of it, and struggled to keep that day alive. Even being shut away every day you dug into that day and pulled out the gold from the bare earth and you lived them in every way you could.

With love and best wishes,
Emma Martin

Emma Martin (age 13), Northamptonshire

Dear Anne Frank,

Although you are no longer alive, the spirit of your diary
and the tenacity of your character have survived as living
beings. They lodge themselves in the minds not only of
those who survived but also of your admirers, those who
have lived part of your trauma through your book and
found strength within its pages. I believe that everyone does
his or her share to remember, either as Jews by going to
temple, or by reading and understanding more so as to
learn history's lessons. Now, at a distance of fifty years we
still remember you. Although I cannot comprehend the full
extent of the war as it took away your life piece by piece, I
try to imagine it by reading about it and by listening to my
great-uncle who survived Buchenwald.

Last August, I went with my family to the Holocaust
Memorial, in Washington DC. The museum was not only
an eye-opener but also a source of neverending discovery;
there were documentaries, live footage and historical
excerpts of the war machine from its beginning to end. It
brought us into the concentration, war and death camps. At
the end of the museum there were two extremely moving
halls. In one room filmed interviews with some survivors
were shown in which they told of their terrifying
experiences. The other hall was a pure empty space in pure
plain white marble, at the back wall of which was an
inscription, and the eternal flame. That one flame signified
the Holocaust and all of those who perished with it. Those
who exited this room were for the most part too moved to
continue through the museum. Fortunately they had the

choice whether to continue or not. While for you, Anne, there was none but to have hope and determination. Your diary symbolizes the lives of those who perished and those who survived. If we want to believe that the power of good is greater than the power of evil we must turn to you.

David Alhadeff

David Alhadeff (age 14), Milan

Dear Anne,

The story of your life was very upsetting for a lot of people, especially myself. I've heard frightening tales about the Germans but none as bad as this. Your story touched my heart and nearly made me cry. I would absolutely dread to live during World War Two. I would not even last one day living inside that lonely, cold and terrifying annexe.

Before the Germans invaded Holland your life wasn't all upsetting. You did everything a normal child would do. You went to school, played outside and went to the seaside. How did you survive? How did you cope? It remains a mystery to some people.

Unfortunately your life had to end in such an upsetting way. Even now you are still known as one of the bravest girls during World War Two.

Yours sincerely,
Steven

Steven Eddie (age 11), Glasgow

Dear Anne Frank,
I like the movies. I like my bike.

I wish you were here and I wish you were not in the sad place.

from Craig

Craig Way (age 7), Somerset

Dear Anne,

I cannot begin to express my sympathy to you, your family and all the other millions of Jews who have suffered throughout Europe. I am currently reading your diary and admire the way you manage, with apparent ease, to string together sentences which I, without a great deal of thought, would not be able even to think of.

Before I read your diary I was ignorant of the torture Jews and their friends went through. Now I have been exposed to the truth I am disgusted. Who in their right mind would dream of wiping out a whole race? Thank goodness the Nazis did not succeed.

I also admire your spirit. Even though it finally broke in the end I do not think that many people could have held out like you did, even for half as long.

I had to laugh at one of your earlier entries (Sunday 21st June, 1942 to be exact). What on earth did you manage to write in the three essays to make Mr Keptor stop giving you extra work? I am sure that I could not write three different pieces like that.

Again I express my deepest sympathy and thank you, for you have shown me what true spirit and bravery are.

Yours sincerely,
Anne Forder

Anne Forder (age 13), Hampshire

Dear Anne,

Now you're dead I can't help you or other Jews. If I had a
wish I would turn the clocks back to World War Two and
I would stop Hitler before he started. But I don't have a
wish so I can't help the people who were hurt by Hitler,
whose lives were ruined and whose families were murdered.

Goodbye Anne
from Samantha Robinson
Your friend forever!

Samantha Robinson (age 10), Cleveland

Dear Anne Frank,

Hi, I'm Monique Robinson and I'm thirteen years old. The first time I ever heard of your diary was when I was about eight. I was in primary school and we were doing a project on the war. I was just a hyperactive little eight-year-old who was never interested in the work and when I *was* interested in the work, I could never understand those big books with all those big confusing words.

One day my teacher brought in these books, they were called *The Diary of Anne Frank*. I took one home and read it and was quite shocked at what I was reading. You were a poor little Jewish girl in hiding living in a world of hatred and pain. You would go to bed at night not knowing whether you would live until the end of the day.

Your mother and the others you were hiding with died, but maybe if you had known that your father was alive you would have had the strength to stay alive yourself. I really, really wish to know what else would have happened in your diary if you had stayed alive until the end of the war.

Rest in peace.

Monique Robinson

Monique Robinson (age 13), London

Dear Anne,

Before I knew the details of your life and how upsetting it was, I just thought you were a girl in the Second World War and died like the other six million did. But when I actually read your diary I did start to understand more, not just how people must have felt during the war but also how wicked and evil the Nazis were. I still don't fully understand about how it was to have a large powerful group of people want to kill me and my people, but what I do understand is that it is not the religion or race of someone that counts, it's the person deep down that matters.

Love,
Belle Findlay

Belle Findlay (age 12), London

Dear Anne Frank,
I have listened to a little bit of your wonderful Kitty diary.
If you lived in 1994 that wouldn't have occurred. You are
such a brave little girl to live in a cupboard only with little
bits of food inside. But I really wanted to say I hope you
died peacefully. I wish you were alive and a little girl so I
could be your best friend.

Lots of love from
Fiona Wilkinson

Fiona Wilkinson (age 7 ½), Otley

Dear Anne,

I know it's weird writing to you, especially since we've never met. I guess it's even stranger, writing to you fifty years after your death, but I have been deeply moved by your diary and the subject will not disappear from my thoughts. The things which you wrote in your diary have made me think a great deal, and it has made me look at life in greater perspective and all the changes which have happened since the war.

Your diary has been read by millions, and I don't know whether it was right to actually publish something which was so personal to you, but your writing has given the world an insight into the Second World War which nobody else could capture, and I feel I need to discuss it. I believe in God, and I believe in heaven, so this letter is written to your spirit which lies there.

I could not even begin to understand how you felt, being stripped of your German nationality because you were a Jew, the injustice of how Jewish people were treated. It's so difficult for me to talk about such horrors which I have never experienced (and I hope I will never have to). We learn in history about the war, the politics, Hitler, the concentration camps – many films and books are made and written about the war. It's a difficult concept to grasp, the fact that what we learn and know as history today, was your reality. I think of you and your family as very brave people who had so much courage for going into hiding. I live as a person who has no worries except for everyday things such as school work and growing up.

I know it isn't any consolation to your death, but you always wished to be a famous writer, and in a peculiar sort of way, your wish has come true. You wished to go on living after your death, and you are alive. Your diary has been read all over the world, and people who read it love your character and charisma which you deliver in your writing. In this way, you are alive in our thoughts and shall never die.

I only wish I had half your talent, wit and charm. This letter was only really written to say one thing to you – rest in peace.

Yours,
Huong Ngo

Huong Ngo (age 13), London

Dear Anne,

Thank you for being like me and showing that ordinary people can be special.

from
Beth Heppleston

Beth Heppleston (age 13), West Sussex